AT THE BASE OF KAATERSKILL FALLS

At the Base of Kaaterskill Falls

Poetry by
Mary Tautin Moloney

Broadstone

Copyright © 2023 by Mary Tautin Moloney

Library of Congress Control Number 2022949838

ISBN 978-1-956782-28-8

Text & Back Cover Design by Larry W. Moore
Front Cover Design by Spock & Associates

Cover painting "Vivi's Ocean"
by Maeve Harris,
used by permission

Broadstone Books
An Imprint of
Broadstone Media LLC
418 Ann Street
Frankfort, KY 40601-1929
BroadstoneBooks.com

for John

Contents

I

At the Base of Kaaterskill Falls / 3
Before / 4
The Raccoon / 5
interior landscape / hummingbird / 6
Damage Reflected / 7
Chrysalis Cracked / 8
Myth / 9
Been Caught Stealing / 10
To Bats who Jam the Radar of Other Bats / 11
interior landscape / fallen horse I / 12
Bottled / 13
To the Baby Screaming on Flight 827 / 14
Northern Lights / 15
To the Hurricane Gathering Strength at Sea / 16
interior landscape / fallen horse II / 17

II

A Study in Suffering / 21
Pentecost / 22
Lazarus / 23
Witness / 24
Moving / 25
Prodigal / 26
The RealReal.com / 27
Little Amerricka Amusement Park / 28
Above / 29
Pineapple / 30
Happiness 31
Stuck on Mariposa Street / 32
Dreamcatcher / 33
The Hows and Whys of Invisibility / 34
Herding / 35
One Mesa / 36
Cog Train / 37
Fall / 38

III

interior landscape / origami / 41
Have You Met my Mother / 42
Auto Correct / 43
Ferry / 44
Stuck in a Bullfight / 45
interior landscape / bandit / 46
Duende / 47
Take Backs / 48
Red / 49
Mariner's Compass / 50
interior landscape / porchlight / 51
Rise / 52
But We Are Not Trees / 53
Glass Church / 54

Notes / 56
Acknowledgments / 57

Everybody knows that they're not where they are.
　　　　　—George Schneeman

I

At the Base of Kaaterskill Falls

My bathing suit is loose from accumulations
of ocean sand and laundry soap, soft and slack

in my hands like an offering. I am a new wife
hidden by the full length of my husband,

pulling off my pants in early autumn. The idea
to swim began with the light: low sun through still-

full trees. It seemed to hold the sudden depth
of water without a lot of questions about *why now*

or *how long*. On the morning of our wedding,
rain bounced from a winter sky. I had envisioned

the kind of current that carries. Still,
the man waited at the altar, like a stag stripped

from the Song of Songs. In the pictures, I appear
transformed, a pearl released and lifted

into grades of deeper water…I see him now
crouched near the surface. And there I am,

on the silent lurch of rock, a breath of a wife.
I stand at the edge, unable to separate falling

from a choice to fall.

BEFORE

Before breakfast, the ocean unfolds
its damage. At the gate,

three birds in a bush. And is it
two in the fist? Flutter distant,

flash of wing. In my body,
baby rolling siren songs.

My mother saw my shape once,
eye tracing cheek. That was all,

that was all, the birds pitch
their call, *What makes us loved?*

Ocean rocked in its leagues.
Belly a muscled stone I touch.

Daughter pressing:
What makes us loved.

The Raccoon

Beneath the table—rustle, eye teeth
closing on my bare foot,
no blood, no puncture and with

little evidence after
my mind reversing the scamper,
flat glance back.

I knew nearly nothing,
white scratch, dusk emerging,
my outline in the window:

mother's cheekbones
stretched and wordless. Darkness
like a hand over the house.

We lived in a coulee, perfectly contained.
After homework, beads of water
where the comb stopped—

what I listened for never came.

INTERIOR LANDSCAPE / HUMMINGBIRD

The way in was never the way out.
Flesh-and-blood drill bit

dumbly turning, conceived from
nearly nothing. Surprising how

the inner world picks up the outer.
Fox tail, brush fire, angelfish.

Hummingbird to drive the mess
forward, sightless. Slate clouds

eat into horizon. How to know
ahead? Canary shore, a spot

to drill against. Surrounding
black, silent life. Hunger.

A breath between.
This deep, no one disbelieves.

Damage Reflected

It was selfish, my love for you;
a vanity—swift and muscular.

Snug within my ribs, you
       were the part
that made me: wife, belly,
threaded needle, whole heart.

Were we joined? I tumble back
and find only damage,
heavy shades drawn.

In this world, I return to the idea
of a bridge across the random tumble.
You are an ancient mouth
stitching in silence.
I pore over eyelets,
the threads you left me.

And I do not accept.

Where is the bullfight of your head
emerging? Heavy shades
released in recognition?

Maybe your mouth is window glass,
damage reflected:
to love

Chrysalis Cracked

Red stains fallen with shell, prints
like pinkie tips. We hit-and-run

oranges through the flap,
our butterfly a sore

muscle stretched. Stillness
when he sips until

one night, porch light burning,
he flings himself at fabric

as if he burns. We figure
it's freedom he wants from this

wedge-sliced world but
unzipped, he stays. Flexes

open-shut. How I sometimes
look back to the terrible

beautiful hatched and turning.

MYTH

I never put birthday money toward
what I wrote in thank you notes. Never

climbed the Blue Ridge Mountains,
I don't know why I said that.

At restaurants, I'm overconfident
splitting the check. I never thought

I'd stop believing in family
as where I ought to be. Six o'clock,

placemats set, milk mostly cold
in a pint for my father, plastic

cups for us, my mother with water
and ice. We held hands before we ate,

to pray. And there were rabbits outside,
in the wooded strip between our house

and the road. I said they were a family
but I never saw them together,

just one or two, not jumping but
stepping carefully, to where there might be food.

Been Caught Stealing

In the beginning, cherries tumbled.
Eve's hair collected pollen

without her knowing; it rose
when Adam pulled his fingers through.

Their steps across a field. The ease.
Kindness incomprehensible.

Eve balanced apples on her stomach
more than once before the bite.

Their skin. Clouds spilled. A mistake
rubbed against so many times the flesh

feels given, trail of black seeds.
Yesterday inside me

my husband whole and hard.
It isn't kindness that has kept us together.

To Bats who Jam the Radar of Other Bats

Selected by nature, a simple
case of survival. Calculations

an overdose dripped. As a kid
I heard your country cousins

banked inside our chimney.
Flapping screaming fluster

wanting nothing but escape.
Now I'm taken by your aim.

Your resolve. Tree limbs
left, ground wheeling.

Once I hid under end tables
faking an escape. Not lost,

not found, years wheeling
like ash. Flapping moth chalked

in your sights. I'll be the cold
under your wing, I'll be the star.

INTERIOR LANDSCAPE / FALLEN HORSE I

Snow falls on the fallen
horse, belly-down in a field.

Flakes fatten, arrowed for
breathing heat. More likely

freeze. Faces in profile
urge the body onward

to the blue railroad's
rulered path. Or away

from broken slogans.
Always the ambiguities.

Black flecks dot the white
as if the horse could rise

up in pieces; as if it could
live as constellations do.

Bottled

Pleiades receded
and dim; ocean
fist over fist, loss

washed in. I swallow,
swallow crave
Sunkist, Fanta,

unnatural sweet,
look for a redo
all my sisters

with me, weeds
rooted. Dinner
cleared, dirty

dishes soaking.
Prince up next
on weekly Top 40.

Our orbits.
Hips bumped.
James-Brown-split

in socks. History
uncollected. Glass
filled with air and flung.

To the Baby Screaming on Flight 827

You lament for us all, trying to be
somewhere else, closer to water

or buildings, to a throng.
You thought I wasn't listening,

but I was. My hands
were also closed like

the time my mother told me
I'm more comfortable being sad.

Here's a story I don't remember:
Little Boy Blue, come blow your horn.

Sheep lost? Cattle strayed?
Look outside: almost night,

violet scattered. Once
I thought a patchwork

made it whole. Now insistent
bloom of pink. You grow quiet.

Northern Lights
Vik, Iceland

Interior empty, deeply off-season.
Nothing carried in my body—

what started went
silent and was scraped away.

Now an open field.
Black pupil, black eye. Expected

and unpromised light
eventually arrived like

Mack trucks hung from a rest stop.
Uneven green across sky.

Then I run from the others,
speak to a God

I don't know. Look up,
wild for a beginning.

To the Hurricane Gathering Strength at Sea

I'm miles below waiting for the slap.
Killing time while power holds

baking bananas turned black.
Against all opposition

nature digs into itself.
You, your growing flank,

eye bulled onto us. Or me,
a child once, inserting myself

on the mattress top before
sheets lowered, wool blankets,

weight settled as my mother
left to change the next set.

Pressure dropped
to dizzy lows. They say

babies may release more quickly
to earth. They warn not to go.

How to not stay? The hope
never to meet you but

the intention to outlast.
Almost humming. Listen.

INTERIOR LANDSCAPE / FALLEN HORSE II

The black horse flares blue,
ears lowered. It must be fear.

Or abandon. Flames
intimate. Tree bark

lowered over itself.
Each trunk a single

painterly stroke. Up close,
the paper of its life.

When this piece breaks—
will this piece ever

break away? White horse
behind the curtain, oblivious.

Arrows whistled, flank
pistoled into night.

II

A Study in Suffering

Imagine a boy, nine or ten, whose job
is to walk west with his family,

alongside a wagon covered by canvas
that grows scarred and smoky, like them.

Smells become food-like as food
dwindles. Campfires cook nothing.

Everyone chews their words—spirited
at first, then plaintive. Then small

and uttered. The boy shrinks
to wheel ruts and cleaves. Lives

in foot falls; lives inside his shoes.
They each recede to the maps

of their bodies. The boy remembers
later, how gnats from the river hovered

his uncovered face. Now,
a different century, scientists say

his children and their children
are heartier and heartier, buoyed

by the boy's thinning. They say
he starved but didn't starve to death.

That the body knew enough
to loosen stones, send them spinning.

Pentecost

18th century, Brazil

I can't remember the details.
Saints carved and paraded: half-

rapture, half-hollow. Priests
weaving streets. I didn't see

up close, the patterns.
Brush strokes. Breeze

through their clothes.
I only saw the display

centuries later. Strategic
light, statues spaced.

I picture mothers and children
knee-down in gravel.

Who craned to see them?
So I return, in the poem.

Find the sculptor's gouge,
a smooth heartwood cheek,

scar ascending like doves.

Lazarus

From the moment her body
freight trained from mine
I was her Lazarus.

Breath given
against my shoulder.
Body its own belief.

Her need spilled
like water
and my hands

there to catch it. Trumping
my pillbox of loss.
Now, late afternoon.

Iced-over yard still spongy
in parts. She howls
from the center, two years

on this earth, wielding
herself like a sword.
Stone that seals.

Stone that rolls away.
World on its platter
coming around, and around.

WITNESS

They turn up without pattern
from thick summer cover;

millipedes, cave crickets
one at a time, with

a busy air, like me in the city
away from my family,

charging *Don't Walk*,
softness a puddle I cross.

It doesn't carry
across the threshold;

my children's small scream
at indifference. I'm beholden

to kill and to save. Hand
lowered, insect arrested,

whole shell nothing but eye.

MOVING

Sightlines crossed almost nightly
through blindless windows,

snake plant potted, baby's milk,
a bottled beer. His bare chest

by fridge bulb, her head
lowered to plates, roots blazing.

Early evening. Unpromised
permanence held to my ear.

Now their truck slung open,
freezer defrosted, man

staring inside. I consider
a wave hello, goodbye. Imagine

my face from where he stands
merged into his own.

Prodigal

One January night, the family dog lost
belly-deep in fresh snow.

My father floodlit as he followed.
Some afternoons, he pulled a toboggan

from dark into day and I'd climb on behind
not sought after but not turned away.

His thick boots catching the hook,
my cheek flush to his coat. We shifted

toward steep pocked with hulls,
grass-flack, flakes broadside, summer

stones bared when we slowed.
My father's face closing its map.

One January night the lost dog was found,
held high and tight to my father's chest.

Floodlit, I put on the story
of the prodigal son. Both brothers.

Servants, pigs. The trough. I would
wander the earth, and never leave.

TheRealReal.com

Leader in luxury—leather, logos.
My real lawn muddied.

Old snow like raw silk
shredded with ice.

I poke at fabric. Add
my sack of loss. The real-real

is a child before sarcasm.
Or sadness chested. Nothing

unravels. I'm freezing,
ditching sneakers for duck boot

stilettos, chunky knits
meant for fishing. I've never

been good at sarcasm. Never
known the thing that makes me real.

Little Amerricka Amusement Park
Marshall, WI

Where iron roller coaster castings
yank neck before gut and kids drive

motorless circles, steering wheel
bolted. Where cemetery stones

slope up a bank while the living
duck into cages, some slightly injured:

knee freshly scraped, molar
hard-packed, ripped paper sack

trailing deep fried cheese, where
fears climb with them, hungers

spin in that small space with them
married to their pasts, however

long or short, over cornfields,
clouds, one cloud belly-out

building into Midwestern burst,
first drop dismissed as figment.

ABOVE

O Earth, dealer in lives
    lovesong of dogs
running roads like a feast
    first angelfish delicate
at the reef. O calm creature,

multiple calamities
    spiked and absorbed
revolver of memory
    longstory written.
O home, I'm waking

predawn facing
    my husband, palm
a leaf to his skin.
    Ridgeline traced. Fingers
slow. Stars dimmed

and slow our bones
    temple, suspend,
wrens release from newly
    crossed twigs depth
shared river quickened

connectors flung. Dark
    sweet. Pulsed furious. Eyes
staid to our heap. Morning
    on another horizon.
O Earth we walk

downstairs lightless.
    He pulls eggs
from the carton, heats
    cast iron. I watch
light arc from your edge.

Pineapple

Where is root and where is stem
with a pineapple? It's like a memory
dislocated. Like a Mother's Day

on the Brooklyn Bridge, when I
maneuvered the meandering,
Manhattan at my back. East River

not a river, despite its name.
I was the pineapple, hurled
from a lawn sparsely planted,

berries burgeoned in the forest
beyond. Back in the day
if a ship survived tropics,

the captain speared pineapple whole
to signal arrival. That May,
under steel girders, sun

and shadow sliced. Hands held
by my children. Crossed
so many times, I became

my own symbol of story
or wealth. Delivered to this place,
and close to whole.

Happiness

Happy is as lucky does and I'm
studying fortune. Its relativity.

Grounded by worse, toppled
by better. The past

a feathered thing. A Rolling
Stones song, the not-getting.

In the happiness study, no single
event ever gives what we want.

Our predictions partial, the stakes
forgotten. For my study I'd take

the tarot card reader at Raoul's.
My past a feathered thing

under her hands. No single event.
No single turn. A hummingbird

at the window. A winged despair.

Stuck on Mariposa Street

In the absence of total absence
what does mourning
loss become? It begins

to feel akin to dumb
like battle cries from cable cars
or pigeons' blank scrutiny.

The Golden Gate lumbers
into its certainty, steel
painted vermilion to blend

with the land, stand
out from the sea.
Beside me, angel's

trumpet flowers, their scent.
A duskywing butterfly
climbing over bark.

Dreamcatcher

Thread she chose: green moss in a creek bed
shaded and cold. Nothing as it seems,

everything tethered to a spot. Potted
orchid, fish tank, its flash of red. Cancer

contained, the gown blue-grey. Thread
woven for her daughters, received and fed.

Beads piled, strays dropped. Nothing tethered,
our toes curled over a swimming pool ledge

last June, our leap. Beaded, sprayed.
Thread green like moss in a creek bed. *Live*

the questions now, Rilke said. We speak
in shallow waves. Nothing as it seems, some

food digested, a walk past every bed.
Lights lowered. The sentence giving way.

The Hows and Whys of Invisibility

It helps to have waiting laundry.
Maternal obligation. To not step

out the door. Not reach for keys,
unlock-unlock so the car

opens entirely out I-95, south
to see if hurricane winds

knocked up the pavilion.
Off-ramp emptied where it's

hard to turn left. Ocean
wintered and steep. Last summer

with my son, beaten gently
in a rhythm, waves stomach-high

until they towered too quick
to show a way through. I lifted

his body, my face silenced.
Clothes dryer chiming. Soft

center exposed. I'm reaching
inside to separate big from small.

Herding

Come-bye, circle one way.
Away to me, then the other.

Come, say good-bye
to who this family

cannot be and go
leave the shears

their yawning grip.
Away, hard-hearted blue jays

against proud snow,
away windows' broken stare.

We're sowing space,
placeholders, gathering

the same dust.
Come-bye, circle one way

past iris planted.
Away to me.

Family wind-borne.
A front moving through.

One Mesa
Point Reyes, California

Across the country, my husband
has become two dreams:

horseman, slow between trees,
and stag at the lattice,

his long low sound. Across
the country our children wake—

I don't know whose cup
needs refilling. My body

has a memory of itself
laid out in forest thick

with swallows, throat lifted.
My husband pulls himself up

over the ledge. We weave
a place in scrub, muscles

mad, bodies steep, morning
breaking open inside us.

Cog Train

  I hear my Beloved

heat from the climb

  leaping on the mountains, bounding

our time in the woods, our skin

  over the hills. My Beloved is like a gazelle

hips muscled, is my feast

  like a young stag. My Beloved lifts—

Mary, will you—

  he says to me, Come then my love

he says my lovely one

  come. My dove hiding

delivered from the clefts above

  let me hear your voice for your voice is sweet.

My Beloved is mine, and I am his.

  He said set me like a seal

love, the flash of it, death

  as strong, a flame

split apart, flood, a torrent.

Fall

Gold-red, drunk purple
up and down side streets

lyrics spilled
between my thighs.

I'm startled.
Delivered to forty,

its verity, lust intact,
details fluttered.

Once I buzz cut my hair
on one side. Once

I ordered pig ears,
learned how to smoke.

Earth on its way
to more of itself.

Revision, ejection, dormancy.
Sweetness at some core

given. My hands
on the wheel, expecting.

III

INTERIOR LANDSCAPE / ORIGAMI

Paper wings show wear,
holes torn by tiny arrows.

Accidental ink
appears wet; intentional

strokes grown dull,
intensity ascribed

to what's darkest.
Glue puddles

from a child's tube,
never fully dry. Fissures

familial. Does color
bleed out, or tunnel

back to the page? To
what's true of the bird?

Have You Met My Mother

My guess is that stars are born,
begin to burn, and don't

look back much. I admire that.
I admire women who fit

stars in their eyes and burn
some light. I only see clearly

with a little night.
If you met my mother,

what did you see?
Maybe the glint from

gravel tucked in a grate,
lodged against air rushing.

It's only a guess. Schedules
I never predict. Double takes,

how it lit. I've heard the moon
runs hot to freeze and holds

onto nothing, which draws me
back to my answerless question

twisted into a shape I can touch.

Auto Correct

Pulled sideways by the sleeve
through Sunday crowds,

roller bag stuffed, balled-up
beach towel wet and cold.

Paperback blotted, small lie
half-disclosed. Numbers

flipping updates where to be
and when; sent up-trail,

upwind, without regard to
weather or companion; without

companion pulled. Not to say
yanked or bulled. It could be

a whisper, buttoned and hooked
as your body bonfires.

Ferry

Lackawanna Terminal like a low-
lying bird, the Hudson between.

My body teetered, healthy.
Routine tests. Three past pregnancies,

two delivered. *And there's age
to consider*, with another conception.

Now sailboats sure in their
sideways course. On the news,

a ship dug up at Ground Zero,
centuries old, artifacts sunk

in muck's layers. Leather
cut for shoes. Birdshot, bones.

Archaeologists scampered
to measure, prayed for more rain.

White oak blinking into metal sky.

Stuck in a Bullfight

Each time it ends with water and a mess
of light. Sometimes I'm the bull

benignly groomed, walking as others walk,
filling my mouth. I feel the fighter,

his easy step. Sometimes I'm him.
Between fights, I lie back to be lifted.

Stare through storm and eye. I'm the bull,
the outflow, last pile of shit. My

existence proven, swag of discontent.
I want flags swinging. I'm the crowd,

gaze split. Sometimes sun unleashed.
But when gates release my body bullets.

Remote, restrained. Then growing
in artistry. Outrageous in beauty.

Intimacy. Dust. A slight weakening.
The fighter's impeccable teeth, words

spoken and impossible. So I crouch
to listen. A kiss sometimes. Or white

stone fallen. Spared, always, the sword's
slack face. Breaking up mud and run,

water and its mess of light.

INTERIOR LANDSCAPE / BANDIT

Midnight masquerade
caught in morning clouds.

The bandit mask
melts inward, sockets

unconvinced. Red scarf
shaken loose. Womb intact,

slap to the face, a gentle
swaddle. Color returned

categorically. Eggs fried,
yolks blurred and lovely.

Light cunning, spread
thin and thick, taken

into black, given over
to shattered sea.

Duende

They're clearing deadwood
from tree crowns, father and son.

Slingshot planted,
weighted rope.

How their cheekbones
angle, re-angle, necks

exposed. Blue jay
aggressive between

lower branches. To enter
thick knots. To enter

a bird's shriek.
Hold maintained—

weed whacker, screen
door, a dog leashed.

Rainwater rushing their faces.

Take Backs

How sure I've been of the ocean.
Always a dark league,

always the moon. If a fish,
the flash through waves.

How one ocean drowns,
another smacks us around

with its wet tongue.
Concession gates lift,

morning cars cross the pier,
cuh-*clunk*. I keep scanning.

Look—blackish seaweed
makes miniature nests,

sand grains the eggs
left unattended. Did I imagine

clam cakes, the roadside stand?
I take back the hands, birds

collected in dunes. My mother
parting, her clean dive through.

Red

The story I make for the cardinal is sorrow,
leave-taking and return, how we

never know what branches will offer.
Throat plush, there's sound—

What do black eyes see? For a moment
I sense it senses me zipped

in skin, husband away for the week.
The story I make

is a clipper ship, I'm hulled by waves.
When he returns I take

off his belt, barely stop to kiss his mouth.
A stain. My dark flush spoken.

Mariner's Compass

What if I love too much
the man who loves me?

Two swans smooth
setting out from the kettle.

Sun rising to its
usual spot. My hands

quieted. His hands
relaxed on the wheel.

There are three types of north
and none point the same.

How to measure. And is that
safer. Lake surface

smoky, how he walks
in a room and I true.

INTERIOR LANDSCAPE / PORCHLIGHT

Fire grows from black
and is contained. Contains clouds,

porchlight moth bumping.
At rock bottom, the drill bit

yields broken pieces.
This story keeps being told.

Fire grown. Small stack of spine,
eye socket, hand opened.

See? Cumulus piled and pulled.
Sunlight dispersed. The angel's

wing whirls, powder
shaken. What appears

to be shoreline is shoreline.
Canary boundary to the thumping.

Rise

In the dream, her heart was a fist of dough.
The secret in its beating: rise, rise.
With each expansion, rivers erupted
dusty skin. Her geography shifted.

In the dream, her seaside neighbors noticed a change.
Some guessed an affair. Others, a child.
The older ones touched their faces. But everyone
felt a longing they had long forgotten.

She longed for the drama of birth, her head
engaged in the pelvic floor. She would move
slowly this time, memorize the muscled walls,
how they held her as she was pushed

away. In the dream, she climbed a mountain path
and witnessed sun, then shadow. Dusk.
Her heart went on its work, losing the scent
of just-created. She missed herself, suddenly,

yeast and yolk. Air rushed from her mouth.
The fist retracted. Her seaside neighbors
noticed a change. Each rose to their longing,
and the longing reduced to a smaller space.

But We Are Not Trees
after Campbell McGrath

Through the window, South Mountain
glows copper. Stockpot filled

three quarters, I toss in salt
with a biblical air. Every evening

this moment of blinding.
Every evening someone

about to come. A squirrel alone
stutters the fence. I never noticed

how expressive the tail; how
removed from its compact heart.

I'm tipping myself toward.
Water in sudden commitment,

squirrel hurtling space. When I was younger
I thought that was us, the thrashing branch.

But we are not trees. We require an act of will.

Glass Church

A wager in a novel: to float the church
downriver. Glass the perfect choice.

It breaks and it cuts—and didn't Pascal say,
belief in God is like a bet? So I make one

with myself to ride the church downriver,
emptied and intact. Cold beneath my feet.

How rare, to cling to nothing.
A body's blush before the bruise.

I'm remembering Easter lilies. *Once
a blind man.* The stretcher lowered.

Mary against Joseph. Narcissus. Anise.
A boy's still-wet hair over his collar

making heads turn, rocks blur. *And also
with you, peace.* Remembering Whitman's

old delicious burdens. *I will toss a new
gladness and roughness among them.*

Notes

The quote by George Schneeman is from an interview with Alice Notley in her book, *Waltzing Matilda*.

"Pentecost" was inspired by the 2002 Brazil: Body & Soul exhibit at the Guggenheim Museum in New York.

"Dreamcatcher" quotes *Letters to a Young Poet* by Rainer Maria Rilke.

"Cog Train" is after the Song of Songs 2:8-17.

"But We Are Not Trees" is after Campbell McGrath's poem, "A Letter to James Wright."

"Glass Church" quotes Walt Whitman's "Song of the Open Road" from *Leaves of Grass*.

Acknowledgments

My gratitude to the following journals in which versions of these poems first appeared:

The Florida Review: "To Bats Who Jam the Radar of Other Bats"
The Florida Review Online: "interior landscape / hummingbird," "interior landscape / fallen horse I," "interior landscape / porchlight"
Quarterly West: "Rise"
Tar River Poetry: "At the Base of Kaaterskill Falls"
Tuesday; An Art Project: "Damage Reflected"

To my friends and teachers at Sarah Lawrence College—to Marie Howe, Victoria Redel, and my advisor Kate Knapp Johnson—I couldn't ask for a more supportive entrée into poetry, thank you.

My sincere thanks to Michael Collier, Jennifer Grotz, and the Bread Loaf Writers' Conference for the Bakeless Camargo Residency where this collection first took shape, and to my fellow writers in Cassis, for the inspiration of their work and friendship.

To everyone who offered feedback and guidance on these poems, especially Fay Dillof, Margot Pappas, Jen Flescher, Jeffrey Perkins, Meghan Dunn, and Diana Khoi Nguyen, thank you for giving me a way out and back in.

Deep appreciation for Ross White and the Grind writing community where many of these poems found their start.

Thanks to my one-of-a-kind Maplewood community and the friends who have taken care of me, made me laugh, and not let me forget my writing life.

To the Loft Literary Center in Minneapolis where I took my first workshop, to my teacher Deidre Pope, and the friends who cheered me on, thank you. Deep gratitude to my sisters, Sarah, Beth, and Julie, and my parents, who never questioned following a dream.

Finally, many thanks to Larry Moore, Sheila Bucy Potter, and Stephanie Potter for sending this book into the world.

And to John, Matthew, and Lauren, the truest base I've ever known, this is for you.

About the Author

Mary Tautin Moloney is a two-time National Poetry Series finalist and a recipient of the 2015 Bread Loaf Bakeless Camargo Residency fellowship in Cassis, France. Her work has appeared in *Tar River Poetry*, *Quarterly West*, and *The Florida Review*, among others, and she has an MFA in Poetry from Sarah Lawrence College.

Mary works as a freelance instructional designer and is a volunteer mentor for Memorial Sloan Kettering's Visible Ink Writing Program.

Originally from Wisconsin, she lives with her family in Maplewood, NJ.